# Parallel Lines

Also by Sue Cook and published by Ginninderra Press
*In Focus* (2016)
*Water Music* (Picaro Poets, 2018)

Sue Cook

# Parallel Lines

For John,
whose homework is reading the poems first.
Now his photos and my poems come together in this volume
in the 58th year of our happy marriage.

For our family:
Michele & Ian, Katherine,
Nicholas, Matthew.
Jason & Deborah, Brooklyn, Jason.

*Parallel Lines*
ISBN 978 1 76109 371 5
Copyright © text Sue Cook 2022
Copyright © internal photos and cover image John Cook 2022

First published 2022 by
GINNINDERRA PRESS
PO Box 3461 Port Adelaide 5015
www.ginninderrapress.com.au

# Contents

# Getting Out

# Parallel Lines

He walks beachwards camera over shoulder
leaving her marooned in the car
in the side street facing the shore.
She's over-ripe, worn out from the relentless heat,
looking out but not seeing the fiery sunset over
Sellicks through the windscreen frame.

All she sees at first are parallel lines:
windscreen edge, far side of road
at the T-junction, a concrete barrier,
remnants of a frail wooden fence,
the thin indigo sea-line of the distant horizon,
low hills, a slight diagonal to her left.

The scraggly tree, a silhouette behind the fence
catches the hot orange ball between high branches,
drops it into low black criss-cross lines,
the smooth sea reflection trembles, fractures,
the sun-ball sinks below the horizon –
a violet band bleeds into pewter-grey sky
changes the naked fading blue canopy –
promising relentless azure for
tomorrow's record temperature.

The lines dissolve into a charcoal smudge
against the grey, the triumphant camera-man
returns, carrying treasure over his shoulder.

# Cloud Music

On a benign autumn day
out for a scenic drive
I think I see above
shiny angels, wings furled,
sitting on ivory pouffes
of cumulus clouds.
They dangle toes
in the sea-blue sky
as they toss invisible
lines over the edge –
fishing for souls
or trout tickling –
through the ether
we hear the glorious
sounds of Schubert's
'Trout' Quintet on the radio
or is this celestial harmony
the voices of angels?

# Wind Farm

The morning landscape is hidden behind a foggy screen
on either side of the highway to Ararat.
Wind is absent and the feeble sun struggles to shine.
Through the ghostly gauzy curtain to the left,
barely discernible, is a long line of wind turbines
across the undulations of a range of shallow hills,
motionless, like actors waiting in stillness
for this last curtain to rise on their sci-fi set.
The windmills await the cue for action
and as the car approaches the low range of hills
there is a faint movement unveiled ahead
as roadside trees and bushes begin to bow and tremble
and from left to right the giant windmills start to move,
switched on by the wind – and so the curtain rises
onstage where the hills are alive with the sound of…

# A Victorian Winter's Day

Frosted farmland stretched wide
like winter washed sheets flank
the road from Daylesford.
Cocooned in the warmth of the car
we travel onwards to the
Westgate Bridge, rearing up
above the Docklands.

Melbourne city is shrouded,
scarfed with murky trails;
yellow windsocks hang limply
above like used condoms.
Traffic, exhausts belching brown
fumes to colour-in the fog,
crawls between sudden stop-starts
(how easy to become car
filling in a truck sandwich).
Gaps in the sullen fog
emerge like missing teeth.
We are spat out at
St Kilda Road, into the cold
dazzling deceptive sunlight
of suburban Melbourne –
Australia's 'most liveable city'.

# Don't Rely on the Sky

that swelling mass daubed with
scratch marks of white cloud
on cerulean blue that morph
into streaks like blond highlights.
Kilometres further along the highway
the temperamental sky ahead
is patched with ominous grey smudges,
leaving tiny blue windows –
fleeting views of skeletal trees
charcoal sketched on the horizon,
the image punctuated by tall trucks –
commas of black crows stud
newly green verges
beside the unfurling road.

# On-trainspotting

We are on a rare train ride into the city
when a young woman leaps aboard
landing, almost falling onto the side bench,
right angled to our double seat, her gaze
transfixed on something distant,
never once looking towards us.

I see a long diagonal scar on her left arm,
frizzy, tired brown hair tipped with red,
dark glasses partly hide a purple bruise.
She's all angles, sharp elbows and knees
those hands wringing, shooting raining blows –
she's dressed for action in black and white,
seeing red: skin-tight white stretch
pants over skimpy black knickers,
black bandeau bra under white midriff top,
white laces in restless black sneakers.

She enacts an aggressive scenario
over and over, muttering incoherent words…
(At first I imagine she is practising her next audition,
doesn't want to say her lines out loud) but next
she wrings her hands, performs a pistol mime,
punishing an imaginary foe, or a lover who's left
her…she murmurs all the while in agitation.

The train slows for the next station…
she paces up and down the platform,
same sequence, still spitting out unheard words,
face screwed up tight in anguish or in anger –
as I look back she's pacing still – pugilistic,
isolated, trapped in her own nightmare.

I take her nightmare with me into town,
I take it home with me that day. For many nights
her anguished face and thin tense body
infiltrate my dreams, colour them black and white,
as my mind still seeks her sad undisclosed narrative.

# Wetlands

I am first in the small car park
but not on the winding path.
A long-legged duck appears
ahead of me, webbed feet
cautious on concrete.
On pond's surface fringed
with bulrushes, two sturdy ducks
power across the water
like mini jet-skis. They leave
a long V-ripple in their wake.
Another adult paddles on the spot,
treading water into widening circles
as she watches her three ducklings,
like bath toys with tiny motors,
weave in and out the rushes.
On my side of the water
grey dirt edges still display
the mud-crazed patterns
of last summer.

# Woodcroft Walk

Follow the red brick path
past the drooping crimson bottlebrush
past a gilded wattle, festooning
a motley jumble of rubbish
mouldering inside plastic, black and green.
Linger at the tempting reserve – shaded by
gangly long-legged gum trees,
weedy grass crunches softly underfoot
where a garden seat for wilted walkers
overlooks a sluggish trickle of water.

A weekday, a benign hush in the street,
no sounds of bees or birds or swish of pushbike.
The bulky olive – green metal box
on the corner is buzzing –
perhaps this NBN node is angry,
its cubic formality breached
by the graffiti of suburban guerrillas.

# Arena Show

Travel weary, dusty, thirsty
on a late August afternoon
we approach the ranges –
distant mysterious shadows
hint at densely treed hillsides,
closer we see serried striations
of khaki, umber, sienna earth
wrap around a bald mountain.
As we near Wilpena Pound the scene
changes, low sun is a moving spotlight
on a stage set of dark trees,
native pines, black trunks thinned out
stretching up from bushy base to peaks –
we are in the colossal auditorium, stage-struck
by the Flinders Ranges Arena Show.

# Back Seat

I have created a nest
in the back of the car
as we three intrepid travellers
negotiate the unsurfaced road
of yet another Flinders gorge.
As the four-wheel drive jolts forward
over stones and undulations
I am imprisoned inside
my own massage machine,
all shook up and facing imminent
strangulation by seatbelt.
Still, the view from the side
of steep scree slopes with
red river gums towering
above the sandy pebbled creek-bed
is far less threatening
than watching the road ahead
from the front passenger seat
where I anticipate constant danger,
stomping on my imaginary brake
as I cry out 'stop, stop' in fear –
what a 'back seat' driver.

# Four-wheel Drive Initiation

The predatory purring of powerful engines
like a lions' pride of four-wheel drives:
there is nothing else here,
except the closed dilapidated kiosk.
In a ragged convoy they rumble off
tuned into instructions via UHF radio.

Sparse scrubby bushes and spindly grass
struggle in salt-white terrain, water lies stagnant
in wheel ruts and holes in the track
under a metallic blue sky.
A sense of utter desolation,
no fixed points of reference –
only the moving vehicles,
the thrumming of engines –
my mind leaps beyond the dry dunes
to the unforgiving outback, lying in wait,

We jolt and jostle over corrugations
crawl up a steep hill, ignorant
of dangers lurking – until we crest, take a deep breath –
plunge down, down onto the muddy tracks
of those who bravely went before.
Later, I drive aslant, driver's side wheels tilted up
on a sand dune, white knuckles gripping the wheel,
a reluctant novice; off air I mutter imprecations
against all the other dauntless drivers –
especially brash four-wheel drive instructors.

# Kangaroo Island

# Kangaroo Island

## The Way to Hanson Bay

At Cape Jervis the *SeaLion 2000*
noses its way out of dock
into Backstairs Passage;
packed vehicle parking space
below, crowded lounge
above, sea-view windows
for hordes of humans:
disparate faces, languages, bodies
jostling and joshing in holiday mode
disembark at Penneshaw.

One road to Flinders Chase
is the South Coast Road to Hanson Bay
traversing the island from East to West.
Road kill has been shunted aside:
kangaroos and wallabies are sad humps,
black crows feast, an eagle hovers.
We pass Wolf Creek and Little Terror Creek,
now and then high revving cars
and motorbikes zip around us but locals
have been absorbed by the landscape;
rubbish bins in gaudy groups
the only signs of unseen inhabitants,
until a black chook with red comb
wanders into view.

Arrival at Hanson Bay Cabins*
is off road onto a rough track,
at the end a sign promises
'Sand, Salt & Silence for your soul'
        deep deep breaths
        solitude and sea spray.

## At Hanson Bay

Eastwards in the bay this morning
the tide is out, frothy water lapping
at dark seaweed edge of whitest sand,
waves curl their fingers out to sea
ready to crash and smash on shore:
foiled, their energy curbed by the breakwater
guarding the bay like some ancient dinosaur,
thin end of tail disappearing into dunes,
rugged head risen above the sea,
rocky sides with giant skin nodules –
the waves are tamed into submission.

Beyond the bulwark of breakwater
in the middle distance to the south-east
the rolling roiling surf pounds
on to vacant biscuit tinted sands.
Further round a distant cape
dunes and cliffs are sea-spray hazy
as if hidden behind a gauzy screen.

* Hanson Bay Cabins were destroyed by the 2020 fires on KI.

As the autumn sun sails higher
emerging from its grey blanket,
a few hardy souls arrive at the beach
(I spy on them from my high window) –
three children fill buckets with sand,
construct a small hillock, a castle perhaps,
add sea treasure, shells, pebbles, kelp
(hard to tell from my eyrie) –
they run around their ragged heap
delighted, clapping and laughing
(the soundtrack is silent for me) –
then flop and flounder in the shallows.

The tide is turning, turning,
sea-water is creeping quietly up the beach…
parents pack up and gesture 'out',
children run, follow up the sand dunes.
The sun has pulled on its grey blanket
as the tide rolls in relentlessly,
cleanses the beach with foamy water,
eradicates footprints, swamps sandcastle,
leaves no trace of intruders.

# Wild West Coast, Kangaroo Island

## Cape Borda

This solid cuboid edifice
squats brooding on the cliff top,
a vertiginous drop down to
the treacherous relentless sea:
Cape Borda lighthouse still dominates
the Wild West coast of Kangaroo Island
but now its great glass eye is closed.
Once the open eye winked its light
across the heaving waves,
rays of hope for ship-weary sailors
and seasick passengers travelling
towards the new colony,
a lifetime beyond England.

## Harvey's Return

Some survived the voyages on the high seas,
on-board disease, menace of rocky reefs and capes;
still sixty wrecked ships wreathe the island,
each a tragedy of lives lost, of abandoned dreams:
another tall ship, later vessels driven by steam,
lying on ocean's briny floor.
Inland a little, away from the crumbling cliffs
is Harvey's Return, a sad and simple cemetery,
names and dates on rough wooden crosses,
bleached and bleak testaments
to the hazards of nineteenth century
maritime travel, isolation of light-keepers,
lost wives and infants, far from home.

## Flotsam and Jetsam

There is a motley museum collection at the Cape,
travellers' expectations dashed on the rocks,
fragments of their hopes and dreams:
a wrought iron letter box, embossed
with a lighthouse pattern, a slot
for letters no postman could deliver,
black wire-framed spectacles, broken
left arm, for reading months old
newspapers from England,
a Wertheim Frankfurt sewing machine
to make new clothes for a new world,
a ceramic sink, Royal Doulton, London,
shards of fine china, willow patterned
and a vase, brown horse rearing, rider
in red hunting jacket, indigo background.
Sea-glass, shape-shifted by the sea
like the bones in the graveyard beneath the waves.

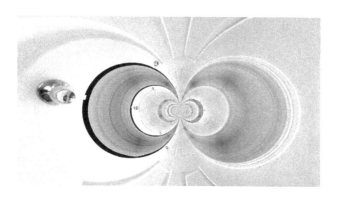

# Asleep and Awake

# Surrealism

On sleep's silent canvas
the routine realist paints
unknowing
with surreal colours
in bold outlines
on the dark background
of night;
fills the spaces with
metaphorical shapes
which resemble day's reality
and, thus dissembling,
inspire with such clarity
visionary patterns,
etch and imprint
the dreaming mind,

leaving
barely perceptible traces
upon the crowded canvas
of a new day.

# Sleep-surfing

Beyond my safe cocoon
of soft pillow bed and blanket
a cranky wind is rising
reeling round the house
slapping the side gate
against the wall behind my head;
a drum tattoo on repeat as
wind whistles and whines
its erratic ragtime jazz
through metal shutters.
With a lull in the soundtrack
hard-won sleep arrives
but I am sleep surfing
neither asleep nor awake –
in the curl of the wave
I reach for the crest
restless on choppy sea,
not surfing but dreaming
in troughs and peaks
until wipe-out at 3 a.m.

# On Edge

On opposing edges
of the marital bed
sideways they lie,
clinging to the mattress
like ship-wrecked sailors
on a broken spar –
no common land in sight.

Softly in the sands of sleep
they stir and roll over,
gently washing ashore
beached like whales
on a sandbank,
warm hands reaching out
across the shingle.

# Tell her she's dreamin'

Wide awake at 3 a.m., my husband fast asleep,
yearning to remember his goodnight kiss
I know exactly what I must do, boot
up my PC, download what I've missed.
I haul myself out of bed, leave
dressing gown and slippers behind.
Stumbling towards the study I stop –
I realise that my mind has filed
the memory, not my sleeping PC.
My muddled brain can't download
this desired piece of data, no more
than it recalls my latest postcode.

# Just a Thought

What if you could grasp
that elusive little thought bubble
before it bursts –
remake it as a lightbulb
moment in your busy wakeful brain.
Wait! This way lies a lot of trouble
if you overload your electric circuits
and flip your safety switch again…
best float awhile on your bubbling thought…
let it disperse into the depths of sleep
from whence your other dazzling notions
have mostly come to nought.

# Sleep Mortgage

Dream-weary and sleep-laden
I rise before dawn ushers in
the challenges of the day.
I have overdrawn my sleep bank again
without saving any credits to sustain me
yet as slotted light peers through the blinds
I push them aside, see the first purple
bearded iris opening in the garden
forget about the sleep-mortgage
embrace the gift of the sunrise –
affirmation of my life's blood
pumping, wiping the debt
off the ledger of night.

# Sleep-writing

I would rather roll over and sleep
than lie awake in a stream of consciousness
like words of James Joyce or Virginia Woolf
rarely hindered by punctuation
in a meandering waterway of night-time thoughts
stopped sometimes by a dam of almost-sleep
but as I seek blissful oblivion
flood-gates open thoughts tumble forth
in words promising much
yet dead by dawn

# Word Wrangler

Firing up the synapses to start reading
a new novel is like diving
into the deep end of an Olympic-size pool
not knowing if you'll sink or swim
or end your marathon journey
too soon, lost in a blockade of words.

Reading a new poem is like immersion
in a deep plunge bath without checking
the water temperature in advance.
On occasion the words scald in their intensity –
you rise from the heat gasping for breath,
other times you plunge into warmer metrical lyrics –
the words lap around you like synchronised swimmers.

Word wrangling with prose or poetry
is like the tourist's venture into new territory.
You sign up unsure of the outcomes – but beware,
reading words is often revolutionary.

# At a Certain Age

She has peaked in her most mature years –
after her ascent of life's steep gradient
this privileged position at its apex
leads her to a mountain top revelation –
it is not the vision of the promised land of Moses
nor the divine vision of racial harmony of Martin Luther King
nor even the 'vision splendid' of A.B. Paterson's Clancy –
rather her epiphany, a realisation, a relief:
no need from now to struggle ever upwards,
nor search for constant footholds on the slope,
no more quakes or volcanic eruptions, floods of tears.
She descends slowly, sure-footed from the cloud-burst
of her summit, in no hurry to reach home base.
As she keeps her frail yet firm grip of the rope
on her way down she wonders,
When will it be time to let go?

# Tidal Affairs

There is a tide in the affairs of men (and women),
which taken at the flood, leads on to fortune…
(With apologies to William Shakespeare, *Julius Caesar*)

A love affair is like a rip tide,
its strong channel of water
flowing from the safe shore
of the home beach through
the surf line of a usual day.

Rip-tide love lifts the lover
faster, higher on breaking waves,
dumps her breathless on the shore
spat out – washed up – washed out.

Safe again in her domestic low tide
ripples of yearning still break the surface
of that ebb and flow of duty, and
turning back the tides of day

she yearns for the moon, earth and sun
to align in a spring tide that she may
rise to a comfortable level of passion
(at least twice a month during the full
and new moon) no longer estranged
on a distant dangerous shore,
swimming into her own safe beach.

# The Unforgiving Mirror

The decades have encroached on Grace
reflected in her draped body and face –
one long look at her mirror image
without its clothing camouflage
shows tree-rings of years like a sturdy oak –
sighing she wraps them in her invisible cloak.
She frowns at her face unmasked by cosmetics,
her brow is etched with wrinkles prophetic
like the sedimentary layers in old sandstone.
Grace lifts her chin, straightens her backbone,
she can still postpone this ageing process,
no one to judge her state of undress.

Next week she'll be the glowing mother-of-the-bride
who will throw these negative thoughts to one side –
on the wedding day she's regal in flowery silk and lace…
smiling back her mirror reflects this amazing Grace.

# The Yellow Dress

Happiness may be intrusive
if emphasised out of context,
an untimely intruder breaching
the fortress of the heart
like a bright yellow dress
shining in the mourning darkness
when others are grieving
the death of father, mother, child
or friend in dull monochrome.
At the funeral a yellow dress
seems too optimistic,
incongruous in the midst
of the black and grey.
Yet a little seed of joy is sown
future gift for those remembering
the celebration of the life that was –
a gift of elusive happiness
waits to be unwrapped.

# Genesis

In the Garden of Eden long ago
Adam and Eve didn't know
the difference between evil and good:
God had created a man named Adam,
from whose rib He next made madam,
Eve, the founding mother of womanhood.

The Garden was inviting, luscious and green,
all around tempting ripe fruit could be seen –
the Tree of Knowledge in the centre stood:
God had forbade them to eat these apples –
but in the dappled light Eve tried to grapple
with such a command, as any girl would.
Eve looked with longing at the Tree –
within the low branches she could see
a serpent slithering round the heartwood –
with fork-ed tongue he enticed young Eve
both God and Adam to deceive
by telling her a terrible falsehood.

Gullible Eve gulped down the fruit,
lovesick and heedless Adam followed suit.
God exiled them from Eden, He'd said He would.
Eve told Adam if only God had kindly said,
'Please don't', but He commanded instead –
a challenge to the first of the sisterhood.

# Falling

Since Eden humans still fall from grace,
not just a dive onto hands and knees;
*'I've had a fall,'* they'll say to your face,
'no one's fault', as if falling is a disease.

Falling or fallen may be words of blame
when they imply a contributing agent:
*Fallen women* are on the game,
how does a woman *fall pregnant?*

*Pride comes before a fall*, moreover,
and thus the stock market rises, *falling*
as proud surefire deals *fall over*
to the sound of investors caterwauling.

As in Genesis, *falling* suggests that our failure is
through an outside source, not our own volition;
a serpent, unseen bump, Covid-19, pregnancy –
indeed falling is the accidental human condition.

# Notes on Time

O let not Time deceive you,
You cannot conquer Time.
W.H Auden

## I Tick-tock

Time is a human construct,
just another way to create
order out of the chaos of life.
Clocks are the outward sign,
an attempt to corral time –
to measure and calibrate
hours, minutes, seconds
lest they run away.
'You can't have too many clocks,'
he said, 'every room needs one.'
But which time is the right time?

## II Asset test

We frown at wasting time,
being too profligate, squandering
this essential life-line credit
as we might regret financial
'getting and spending'.*
We worry about time running out
as if we can tame transience
into something finite:
'Time is money,' he said.

* William Wordsworth, 'The World Is Too Much With Us'

## III Rubber band theory

Despite our obsession
with keeping time
we cannot control it.
Time is like a rubber band,
stretching almost without limit
in childhood (remember those
warm summer school holidays)
but as we reach our middle years
ambition, work, relationships…
that band starts to stretch and strain –
assets rich, time poor.

## IV The time is nigh

Elasticity is str-etch-ed into
maturity, regulation, old age:
even in retirement some cry
'I don't know how I found
the time to go to work.'
The rubber band hardens
as arteries lose plasticity,
the circadian rhythm falters,
the internal clock stops.

# Staying In

# Out of the dark...

The weatherboard house is pole-tethered half-way up
the slope of dried grass, summer fires threaten again –
inside, rooms are darkened by towering blue gums
planted with youthful enthusiasm 47 years ago;
swathes of curling bark litter the ground and branches fall,
one killed a koala on a hot and windy Australia Day.
Like the prow of a sailing boat, the back deck rises high:
cockies screech, argue over feeders, white-bomb the floor,
bejewelled lorikeets wait and gossip on the Hills Hoist
while magpies in dinner suits eat a smorgasbord below.

Inside, estate agents inspect, evaluate, tap walls, murmur
*It's so seventies*...so are we, don't want to be fenced in
by 'Good Neighbour' steel, a manicured garden, a house
without character...then, a whisper on the wind,
*flat ground, no more mulching bark, no stairs*...louder,
*no more hard yakka*...insistent, *time to smell the roses.*
South we go to hunt houses, some too small, some too big,
we feel like *Goldilocks*...but now mature roses beckon,
pink out front, glowing gold next to emerald green fernery,
warm apricot on the other side; the house itself is *just right,*
windows frame garden views on three sides, maggies forage,
we move into the light...

# Home Library

There is no real need for diction
when you read a work of fiction
silently to your own good self.
But there may be marital friction
about my fiction inclination
crowding out his volumes on the shelf.

In our library there's some quandary,
indeed it's quite reactionary,
about which books should be displayed.
His works of science and discovery
push my volumes to the periphery,
ignoring how I like them all arrayed.

You could argue with conviction
that a bloke who reads non-fiction
doesn't know what real reading is about;
he considers love of poetry and fiction
a most strange and puzzling affliction,
one he's more than happy to go without.

Then one day there came the great eviction
of so many books without restriction,
for we had to cull them when moving house.
I packed the book boxes as was customary,
sent his books to the periphery –
this time no quibble from my spouse.

# Outside the Box

Crammed into corners
like stacks on the mill
the boxes rise high
in cardboard towers.
In our packing frenzy
contents labels
become Texta scribbles,
indecipherable as
Egyptian hieroglyphs
when parked in the new house
by weary removalists.
On the outside our labels
defy interpretation –
the only solution is to open the box,
reveal the hidden trash or treasure.

# Talk

A full family meal in Melbourne,
grandchildren one, two, three,
all over 20 but under 30, parents
not yet 60, cooking up a nutritious storm
on the other side of the island bench;
some for newly vegetarian offspring
meat for the rest of us carnivores.
All of them talking, talking, talking
in soundbites like a live version
of Twitter or perhaps Facebook…
no time or sound-space for
elders' long winding narratives…
unwittingly cut across or cut into
by the artless babble of siblings
reunited for this family meal,
short story morsels from uni lives
garnished with social titbits.

A dilemma for grandpa
closely watching the eager young
faces to see what they're saying…
he tries to assemble these
verbal jigsaw pieces and
chimes in for his say after
the general gist has changed.

They listen and try to put him on track,
but these horses soon gallop away.

Home again he returns to his silent
1,000-piece jigsaw puzzle
in soothing greens and blues,
no missing parts.

# BC to AC

*January 2020 BC*
Before the great coronavirus lockdown
we would both go forth to forage
for essential and delectable fodder
in supermarkets overstocked with foodstuff;
amid teeming aisles of overabundance,
spoilt for choice we'd amble at a gentle dodder.

*March/April/May 2020 DC*
I send out my hunter-gatherer
early in the morning to seek our sustenance –
empty shelves are rebuff enough
to hoarders who exceed the allowance
of staples: flour, rice and that paper stuff,
yet home from the hunt he returns in triumph,
my canny fodder plodder.

*June/July and beyond 2020 AC*
A new normal? Perhaps, perhaps, perhaps…

# Blue Wash

Adelaide July 2020

This morning the winter sky
is a washed-out faded blue
as if the master painter
has diluted his summer palette.
Diminished by the winter chill,
despite the fraudulent sunshine,
people in all the states of the nation
sense waves of deepest indigo wash over
them as corona virus strikes hard again…
Melbourne city is slammed shut.
Families and friends back in lock-down
joyful celebrations side-swiped:
weddings, wakes, significant
birthdays and even local barbecues –
haunted now by ghosts of parties past.

# Colour me in

## 2020

Each day is another page of strange
patterns in my annual colouring book;
some shapes are already filled in
with recurring purple and pink spheres,
nodule-dotted, framed in blue rectangles
trespassing on monochromatic swirls:
smudged charcoal, murky greys, ashes
of anxiety, depression, uncertainty.
Sometimes the dangerous red of anger
bleeds into these cheerless shades…

## 2021

This year I will colour-in a new book,
soothing, clear shapes of promising
designs – circles, squares, ovals,
open spaces – softer pale pastels
and gentle greens amid the clear white
of peace and better health
in a recovering world.
Wishful thinking,
new purple and orange pimpled balls
are now invading the blue rectangles…

# Anxiety

is like a paring knife,
at first blunt and barely scraping the brain,
then sharpened by the whetstone of events:
Covid-chaos has people in disarray:
lives lost, final goodbyes missed
through lock down rules, border closures;
funerals functional, minimum mourners,
joyful weddings postponed into an uncertain
future, but no dancing cheek to cheek.

The world holds what breath is left
as it waits for the miracle vaccine
to create order from anarchy and
let all those in isolation reconnect
as states and nations open borders –
global anxiety retreats like a whipped
dog that lies in wait, ready to return
when the next pandemic beckons.

December 2021

# Hitchhiker

I see distressing images of wretched refugees
beating at the closed gates, that hostile barricade –
no longer welcome in the USA, not safe in Venezuela,
desperate, fleeing north from the despot's rule –
this mass exodus doomed to rejection.

I read of the annual migration south of monarch butterflies
escaping from the chill of the northern American autumn.
The newspaper tells of how a lone ranger butterfly,
compelled by instinct, flaps flimsy wings in a fickle wind
drops still fluttering orange, black and white
onto the path of a sharp-eyed cyclist.
At home, she gently tends the crippled monarch,
repairs its damaged wing, persuades an amiable
southbound trucker to take this fragile passenger
on the long odyssey to warm Florida…freed and flapping
both wings the lone ranger heads further south,
seeking the critical mass of seasonal immigrants.

Today on screen I see more confusing images –
resigned, sad and far too skinny people massing
together in borderline camps in their thousands,
refugees from war zones grounded, doomed,
no fight or flight left, hope in scant supply.

# At Easter Time

## 1. The Arrest

Words, words, words.
How much depends upon words.
People chattering, agitating, politicising,
gabble, gabble – traitor – gabble, gabble – pretender.
With swords and clubs they press in
to arrest Jesus.
Judas says, 'Peace be with you teacher',
betrays him with a kiss.
The high priest accuses him of false promises
but Jesus is silent.
'Are you the Messiah, the son of God?'
'You will see the Son of Man sitting
at the right hand of the Almighty.'
Blasphemous words seal Jesus' fate.
More words – Peter denies knowing Jesus –
no, no, no – and the rooster crows.
Pilate demands more words from Jesus and gets none.
He asks the rabble what to do with the Messiah
gabble, gabble – crucify Him – gabble, gabble.
Words, words, words.

## 2. Crucifixion

A dark day indeed
when they come to Golgotha,
the place of the skull.
Blackness inside people's hearts
as they watch the crucifixion unfold.
Soon, shrouded in darkness
Jesus is isolated, suffocating,
there is no light, no enlightenment,
the darkness is impenetrable.
He hangs, abandoned by man and God:
'My God, my God, why have you forsaken me?'
Jesus dies on the cross
as the women watch from a distance
lamenting this death of the One
who has given them new life.

## 3. Resurrection

As Sunday morning dawns
and rosy light dissipates darkness
the women approach Jesus' tomb,
mourning their inconsolable loss.

Suddenly, they are bedazzled
for a bright angel irradiates the cave
where Jesus was entombed;
'He is risen, elevated, raised from death',
and the women rejoice.
Angel or hallucination?
In wonder, Mary Magdalene
plucks a white feather
from the ground.
Jesus appears to these faithful friends,
preaching peace and lack of fear,
meets the disciples, too, in Galilee.

Out of the darkness into the light,
so are we all illuminated
by His death and resurrection.

# Easter Monday

Adelaide 2020

A mellow Keatsian morning –
as if Nature herself is responding
with extra kindness to soothe
our locked-in, locked-down isolation
from the comforts of human touch.
A playful breeze ruffles
her lush green skirt, embroidered
with nascent cyclamen, a deeper pink
than summer roses that linger, petals
floating down to mingle with the eager
green shoots that brush her hem, rising
with hope for an open-house spring.

I tune in to the joyous violin sounds
spiralling ever upwards in the liquid notes
of Vaughan Williams' 'The Lark Ascending' –
almost as if Nature has ordered this music
as an antidote for shut-in, shut-down souls,
promising an exultation of larks, a rise in spirits
in the wake of Resurrection Sunday.

If not larks for us in our southern spring
we can look forward to congregations
of magpies warbling their matins chorus –
rousing us from sleep and the long
'winter of our discontent.'

# After the Rain

February 2020

My garden is deliriously drunk – on water,
a sudden summer deluge from on high;
the young pittosporums are clearly tipsy –
they tremble, lean into each other and sigh.

The mandarin tree sags low
with fruit and water-laden leaves.
Pink petunias, pansies and primulas
droop downward on their knees.

The flowering fuchsias flop around
as if they've been out on the town,
while the violets are suddenly perky,
no longer parched and turning brown.

Blue lobelia's been languishing
but now is plumped and spry,
bejewelled maidenhair fern shakes
her tresses, rejoices after the long dry.

Potted geranium boldly flaunts itself,
flushes bright red after such a binge.
Coriander, parsley and oregano sprout
as they no longer need to whinge.

If only this wondrous rainfall would
drench places wretched with drought,
water farms, fill creeks and ease the pain
of those who've been so long without.

# Climate Change

If you believe in an awesome Deity
you may not expect spontaneity –
yet famine flood and forest fire
tempest and turbulence dire
may seem akin to punishment
by the God of the Old Testament –
thunder-sent to make you pay
for all of us who disobey.

On the other hand, you may pause –
if you believe in a human cause
(you'll do your best with solar power
resolve to take a shorter shower)
though environmental destruction
may seem like spontaneous combustion –
either way we appear to be
destined for catastrophe.

Yet the environment would argue back
that earth has long been on this track
of devastation and natural disasters
predicted often by climate forecasters -
thus we turn to these new prophets
and corporations who make profits
harnessing the elements for clean energy
to benefit earth and its human family –
when what we seek are seminal signs –
God   Humanity   Nature
in serious synergy.

# The Farmer's Tale

Across the land it is the big dry –
No clouds in the relentless blue sky.
Shrivelled crops on thirsty ground –
Relief is nowhere to be found.
Savings swallowed into a black hole
Of debt and farm machinery sold.
How can he stay and work the land
When it can't support his loving clan?
His wife looks careworn before her time –
His children's clothes are covered in grime.

Driven towards the dark abyss –
He is listless, luckless, life is cheerless.
Head in hands he rues the day
The drought began to make him pay.
Alone he contemplates the past
And now a future looking dark.

The summer heat leaves topsoil parched
Whirlwinds whip it up in March
Still no rain, the earth is silent
Thoughts of ending life are rampant
Desolate his thoughts turn inward
Could he-would he-be a coward?

Upon his door he hears a knock,
Listens, sighs and checks the clock.
His daughter enters, face alight.
She says, 'Dad, it rained last night.
Come outside and smell the air–
Rain is soaking ground so bare.
Mum says the crops will shoot again
And we won't have to suffer pain.'
She takes his hand and leads him out,
Squelching mud, he cannot doubt,
And when he raises eyes up high
There's a rainbow arch in a new grey sky.

Recovery will be slow he knows
But the promise the radiant colours show
Breaks through drought and dark despair –
At last, a response to his fervent prayer.

# Last Rites

After the Melbourne Museum exhibition, Tutankhamun and the
Golden Age of the Pharoahs, 2015

On a Ptolemaic funerary chest intricate
hieroglyphs and decorative symbols entwine
to tell the life-story of the departed;
fifty faience carved *ushabtis* serve their master,
eternally faithful, attuned to every need.

A sun worshipper erupts from stone,
arms raised to the glowing sun,
symbol of eternal resurrection
illuminating the long sleep;
divine images cluster on coffins,
invocations against the inevitable
descent into oblivion or decay.

Egyptian obsequies seem long, leisurely –
at ease with life's final paradox –
crafting connections, shining through grief
with sun's promise, optimism eternal.

Today's last rites seem more perfunctory,
less time for outward lamentation:
funeral craftsmen now are undertakers,
Facebook posts are hieroglyphs,
coffins plain polished, ephemeral flowers –
mourners linger awhile with the eulogy,
shed a tear or two with the requiem
(favourite music of the recently departed)
then make a speedy exit and farewell.

Some linger…still offering silent
prayers to their god or ancestors
for the miracle of meeting again
should life be eternal
and the dead become divine.

# In Memoriam

Let us think upon current wokeness –
of bronze figures brazenly toppled
off pedestals, of cast-iron sculptures
of pre-woke Western leaders,
reduced to scrap metal in skip bins.

Now, see the bust of comrade Lenin,
a revolution remnant found in Antarctica
at the remote 'pole of inaccessibility',
his stern frozen likeness
planted there during the Cold War,
gazing steadfastly towards Moscow.
After seven years, a US research team
turns Lenin to face Washington
but Soviet scientists turn him back.
Never revoked by political correctness
this Lenin has escaped the iconoclasts
only to suffocate and slowly disappear
in winter's rapidly rising snow levels.

# Contemporary Christmas

Welcome wreath on door
spangled tree inside
wrapped gifts beneath.

Greeting cards from far and near
reaffirm old friendships
like an annual handshake;
>            amid festive images
>            bells and baubles
>            all gold and glitter
>            snow and Santa Claus
>            trees and tinsel
>            red white and green –

a 16th century painting by Raphael
shines like a beacon,
illuminates the nativity,
the first Christmas.

# Gift Wrapped

In the ebony sky
a radiant star beckons to the faithful,
heralds God's gift of the infant Jesus.
Wise men follow the star bringing gifts
of gold, frankincense and myrrh
to a baby much too young
to understand their import.
He gurgles at the sight of these exotic princes,
turns to his mother Mary for comfort.
The watchful shepherds are silent, awestruck.
The gifts are wrapped in gold and silver silk,
opulent and at odds with the baby
wrapped in plain blue cloth,
displayed in a straw-lined box:
a much more modest package,
God's eternal Christmas gift.

# Acknowledgements

Ginninderra Press anthologies:
*Wild*, 2018, 'Initiation'
*Mountain Secrets*, 2019, 'At a Certain Age'
*I Protest, Poems of Dissent*, 2020, 'Hitchhiker'
*Milestones*, 2021, 'Out of the dark…'

*The Crow*, Ginninderra Press, editor Joan Fenney:
'Huck's Lookout', 'The Yellow Dress', 'In Memoriam'

*Friendly Street Readers*:
#41, 'Surrealism'
#42, 'A Victorian Winter's Day', 'Tidal Affairs'
#43, 'Home Library'
#44, 'On-trainspotting', 'Sleep Writing'

ELC Anthology, *From Our Desks*, 2020, 'Don't Rely on the Sky'

*Poetry Matters,* editor Cheryl Howard:
'Retrieval', 'Watermarked' ('Watermarked' republished in final *Poetry Matters*, Issue 40, 2020, Democratic Poetic), 'Parallel Lines', first published November 2019, 'Woodcroft Walk', 'Arena Show'

*Oxygen*, editor Cheryl Howard, Issue 1, 2021, 'Sleep Surfing'

*Studio*:
#146 'Last Rites'
#148 republished 'Parallel Lines' (see above *Poetry Matters*), first published 'On-trainspotting'
#152 'After the Rain', 'Easter Monday'

*tamba*:
'On Edge', 60th Anniversary Issue, Autumn/Winter 2017
'Wind Farm', Autumn/Winter, 2019
'Word Wrangler', Spring/Summer, 2020

*The Mozzie*, various issues, 2020–2021:
'Tell her she's dreamin'', 'Sleep Mortgage', 'Back Seat', 'BC to AC', 'Blue Wash', 'Colour me in', 'After the Rain'

*Positive Words*, various issues, 2018–2020:
'The Farmer's Tale', 'Genesis', 'Just a Thought'

*The Write Angle*, 2018, 'Climate Change'

'Poets Corner', *InDaily* online, 2017–2021:
'A Contemporary Christmas', 20/12/17,
'Kangaroo Island: The Way to Hanson Bay', 7/9/18,
'Kangaroo Island: At Hanson Bay', 14/9/18
'Cloud Music' & 'Wetland', 11/4/20
'Wild West Coast, Kangaroo Island', 22/4/20
'The Unforgiving Mirror', 6/2/21

CPSIA information can be obtained
at www.ICGtesting.com
Printed in the USA
LVHW040900240822
726654LV00010B/938